Love Protects: The Armor of God

LOVE BEYOND BORDERS

Ruth Ella Wilson

illustrated by
Nikki Weiman Rogers

Trilogy Christian Publishers
A Wholly Owned Subsidiary of Trinity Broadcasting Network
2442 Michelle Drive
Tustin, CA 92780

Copyright © 2019 by Ruth Ella Wilson

All Scripture quotations, unless otherwise noted, taken from THE HOLY BIBLE, NEW INTERNATIONAL VERSION®, NIV® Copyright © 1973, 1978, 1984, 2011 by Biblica, Inc.® Used by permission. All rights reserved worldwide.

Scripture quotations marked (KJV) taken from The Holy Bible, King James Version. Cambridge Edition: 1769.

All rights reserved, including the right to reproduce this book or portions thereof in any form whatsoever.

For information, address Trilogy Christian Publishing

Rights Department, 2442 Michelle Drive, Tustin, Ca 92780.

Trilogy Christian Publishing/ TBN and colophon are trademarks of Trinity Broadcasting Network.

For information about special discounts for bulk purchases, please contact Trilogy Christian Publishing.

Manufactured in the United States of America

Trilogy Disclaimer: The views and content expressed in this book are those of the author and may not necessarily reflect the views and doctrine of Trilogy Christian Publishing or the Trinity Broadcasting Network.

10 9 8 7 6 5 4 3 2 1

Library of Congress Cataloging-in-Publication Data is available.

ISBN 978-1-64773-265-3
ISBN 978-1-64773-266-0 (ebook)

Ephesians 6:10-17 (NIV)

"Finally, be strong in the Lord and in His mighty power. Put on the full armor of God so that...you may be able to stand your ground, and after you have done everything, to stand. Stand firm then, with the belt of truth buckled around your waist, with the breastplate of righteousness in place, and with your feet fitted with the readiness that comes from the gospel of peace. In addition to all this, take up the shield of faith, with which you can extinguish all the flaming arrows of the evil one. Take the helmet of salvation and the sword of the Spirit, which is the Word of God."

Thank You, God, for giving us special clothes.

We put on this armor every day and wear it everywhere we go!

¹⁰ "Finally, be strong in the Lord and in h[is]
God, so that you can take your stand ag[ainst]
is not against flesh and blood, but against
powers of this dark world and against
realms. ¹³ Therefore put on the full [armor]
[so that] may be able to [sta]nd your gro[und]
¹⁴ Stand firm then, [with] the belt
br[east]plate of righteousness in place [and]
co[me from] gospel of peace.
w[ith]... can extinguish all the fl[ames]
of [...] the sword of the Spi[rit]
Spirit on all occasions with all kinds
alert and always k[eep on] praying for
whenever I speak, words may be giv[en]
m[ystery of the] gospel, ²⁰ for which [I am]
declare it fearlessly, as I should.

Sword of the Spirit

Breastplate of Righteousness

Readiness that comes from the Gospel of Peace

Helmet of Salvation

Belt of Truth

Shield of Faith

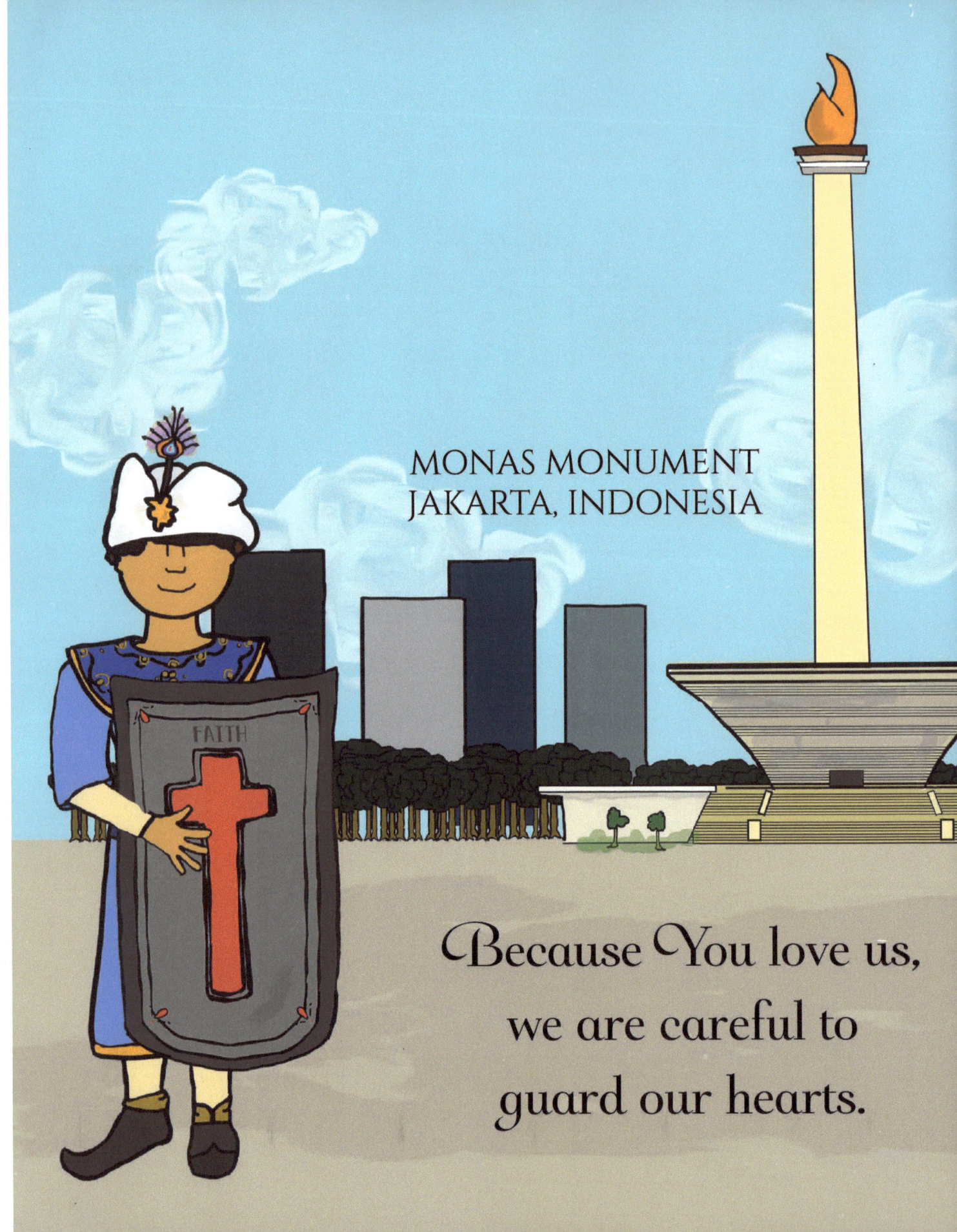

We carry the shield of faith to protect us.

CHRIST THE REDEEMER
RIO DE JANEIRO, BRAZIL

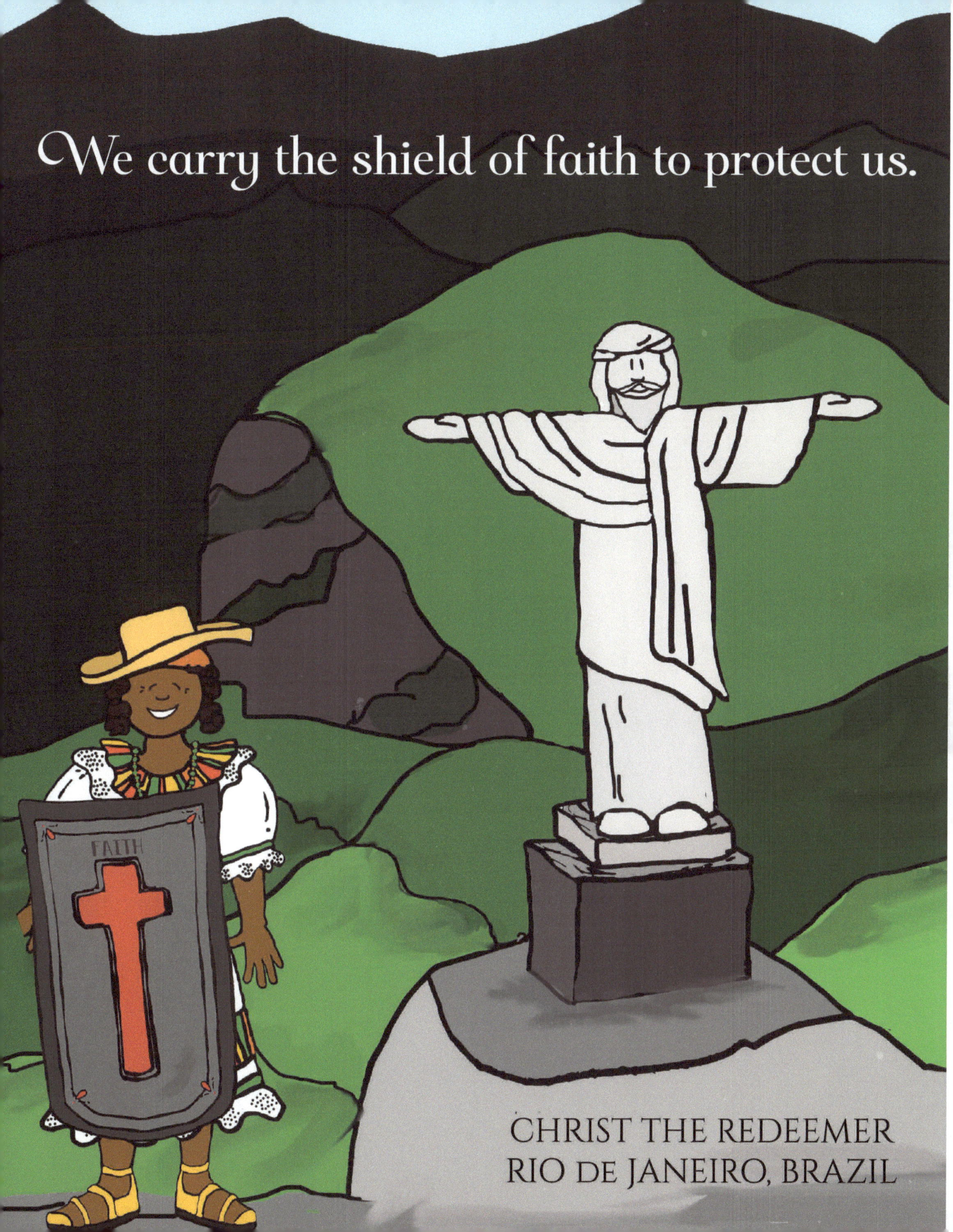

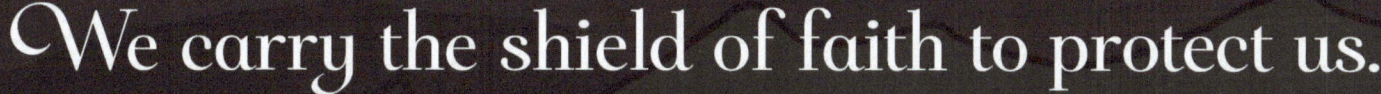

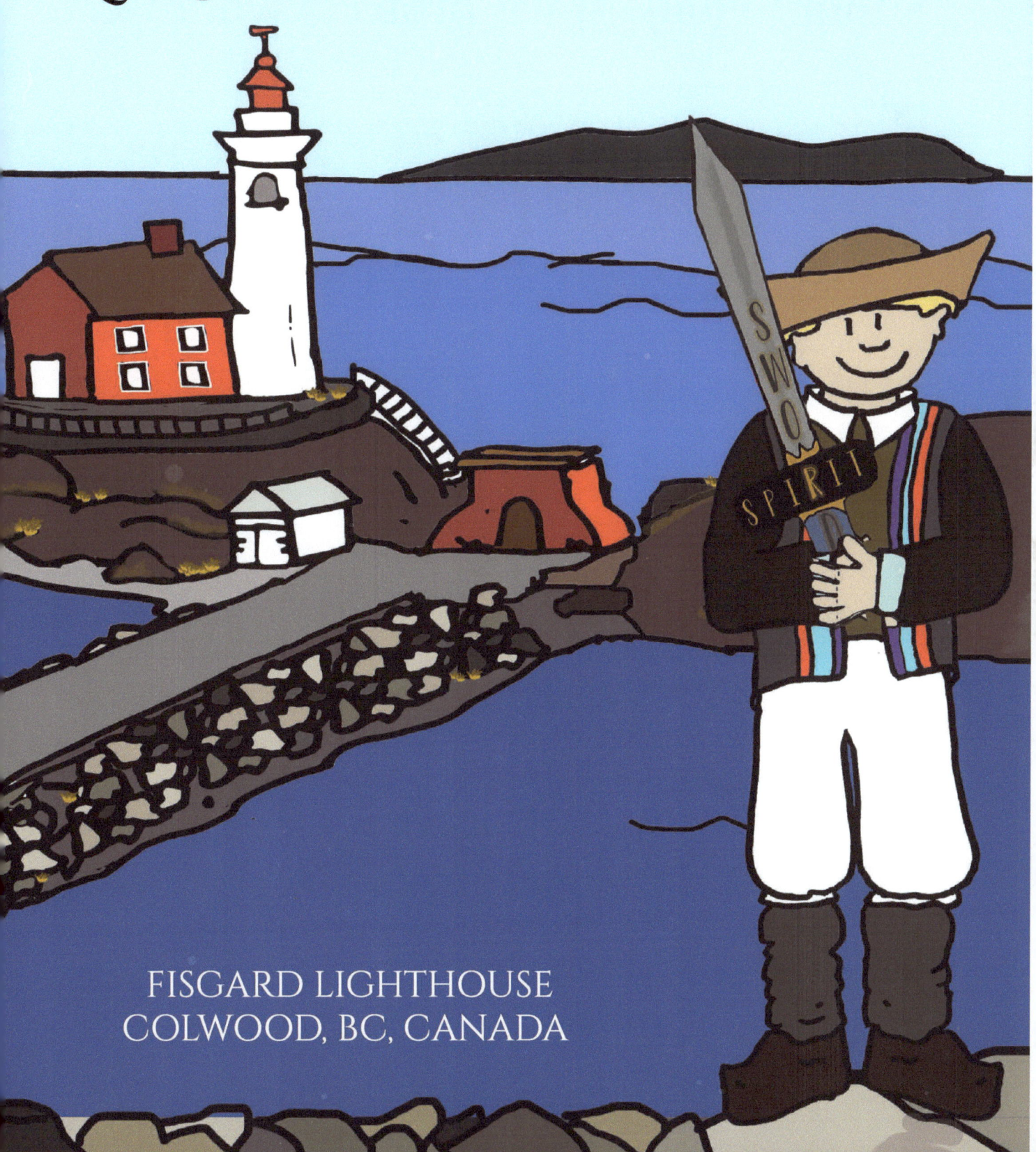

Because You love us, Your Holy Spirit protects what we

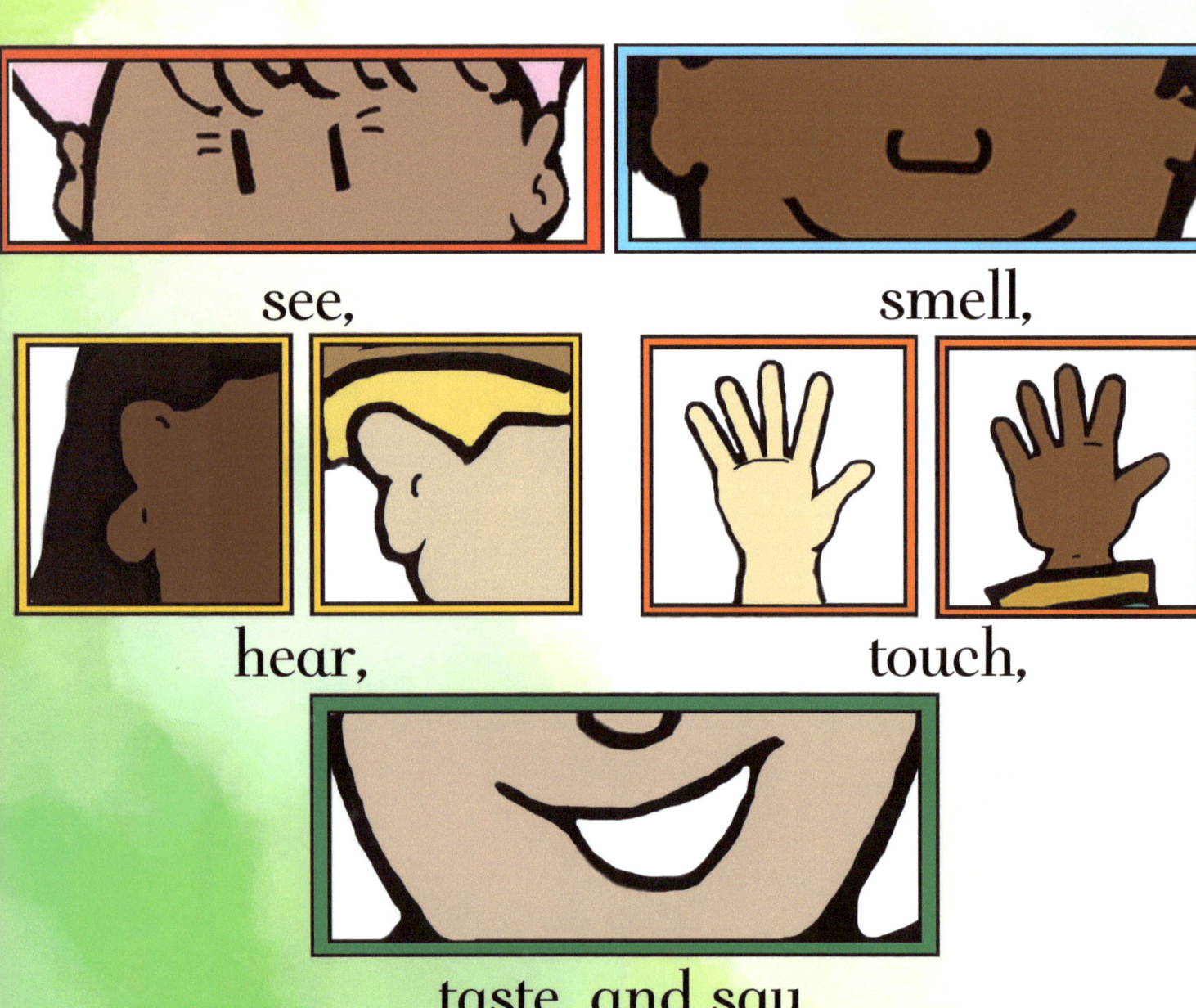

see, smell, hear, touch, taste, and say.

We thank You, Holy Spirit, for protecting our mind, body, and spirit.

What makes you feel safe?

How will you help others feel safe?

CPSIA information can be obtained
at www.ICGtesting.com
Printed in the USA
BVHW021738070521
606754BV00010B/358